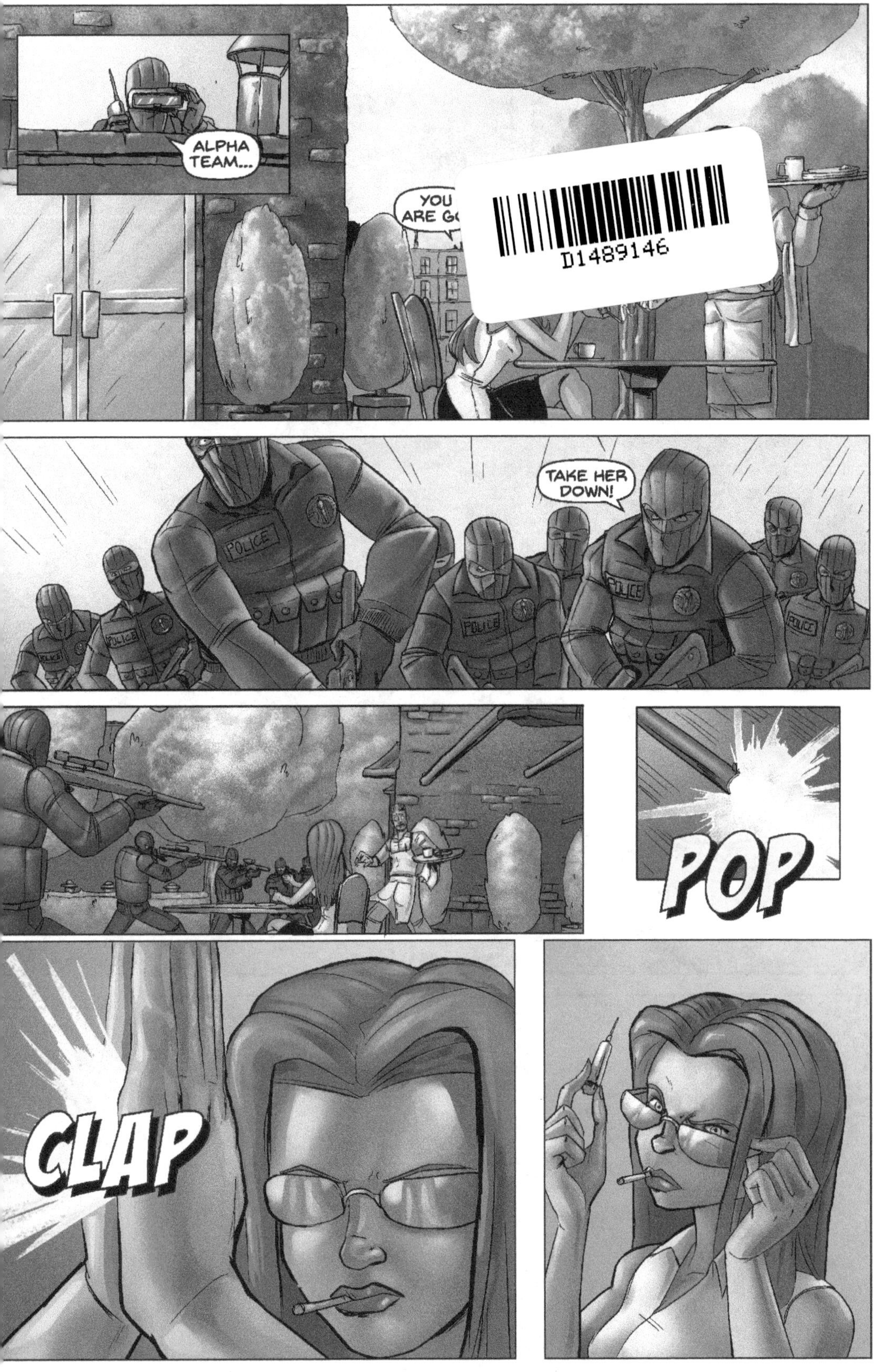
ALPHA TEAM...
YOU ARE GO
TAKE HER DOWN!
POP
CLAP

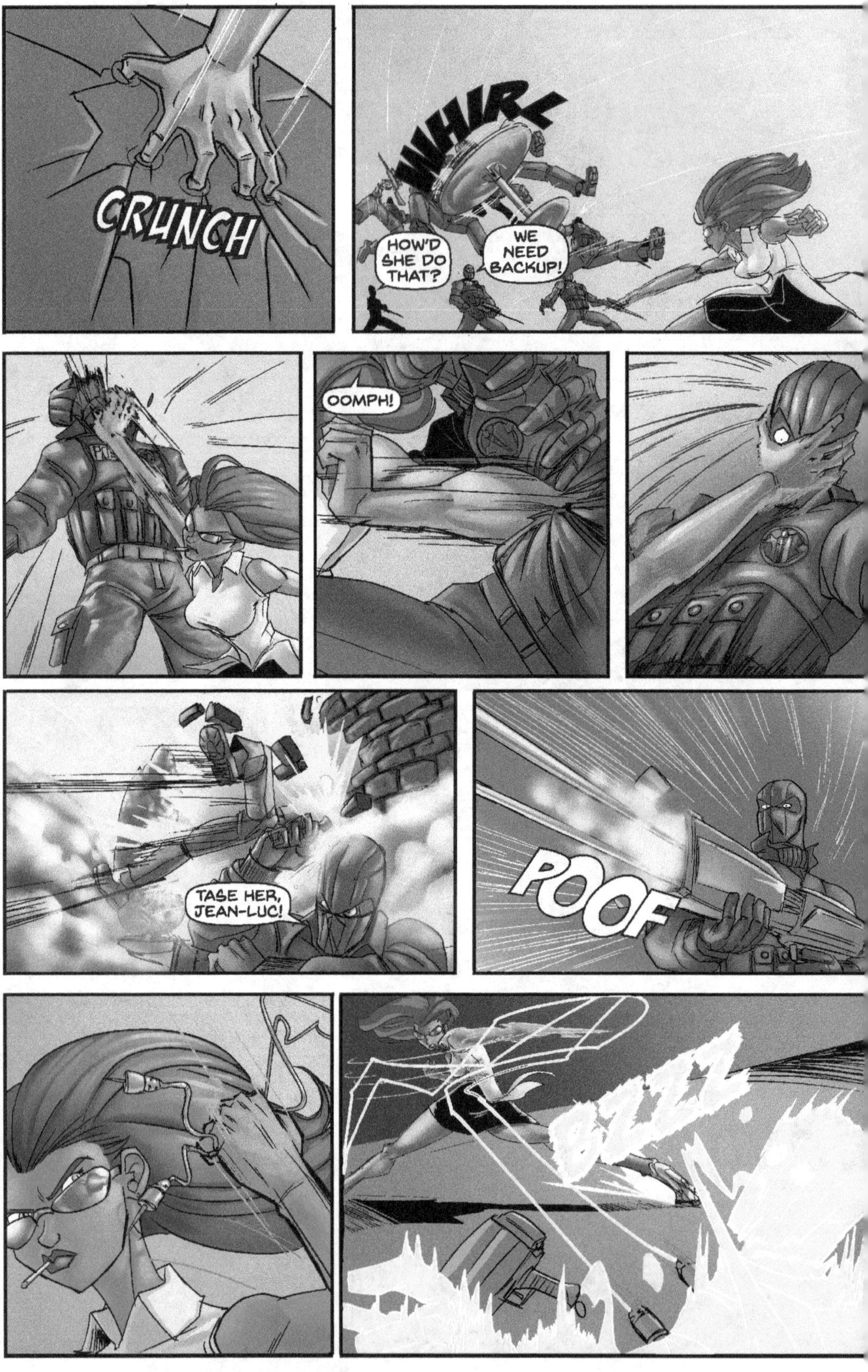
CRUNCH
WHIRL
HOW'D SHE DO THAT?
WE NEED BACKUP!
OOMPH!
TASE HER, JEAN-LUC!
POOF
BZZZ

STAND DOWN! LET HER GO. THE CAPTAIN WILL TAKE CARE OF HER.

WHOOSH

EEYYAARH!

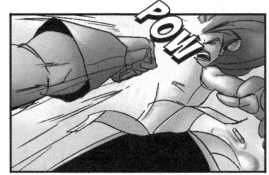

POW

BOOM

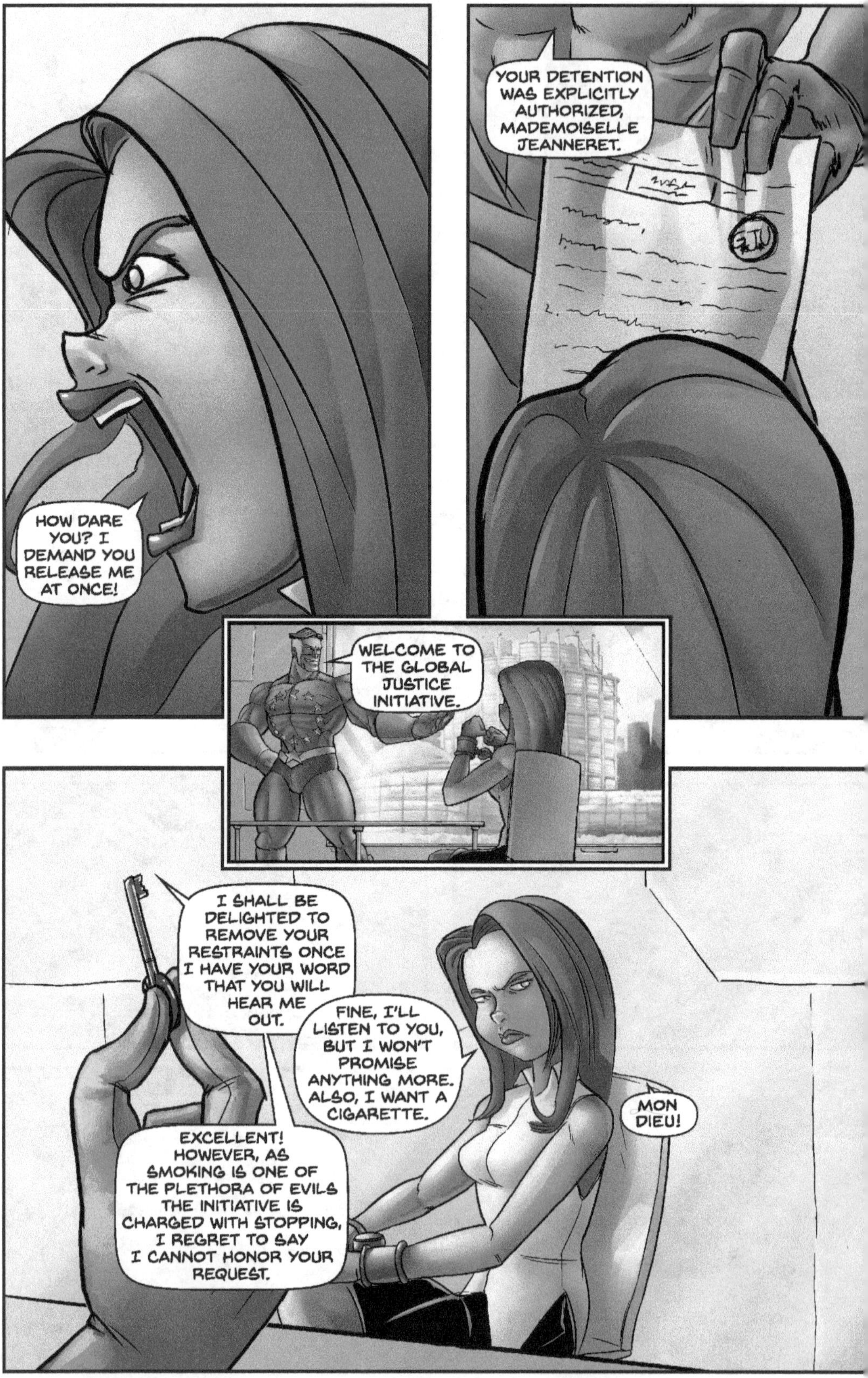
HOW DARE YOU? I DEMAND YOU RELEASE ME AT ONCE!
YOUR DETENTION WAS EXPLICITLY AUTHORIZED, MADEMOISELLE JEANNERET.
WELCOME TO THE GLOBAL JUSTICE INITIATIVE.
I SHALL BE DELIGHTED TO REMOVE YOUR RESTRAINTS ONCE I HAVE YOUR WORD THAT YOU WILL HEAR ME OUT.
FINE, I'LL LISTEN TO YOU, BUT I WON'T PROMISE ANYTHING MORE. ALSO, I WANT A CIGARETTE.
EXCELLENT! HOWEVER, AS SMOKING IS ONE OF THE PLETHORA OF EVILS THE INITIATIVE IS CHARGED WITH STOPPING, I REGRET TO SAY I CANNOT HONOR YOUR REQUEST.
MON DIEU!

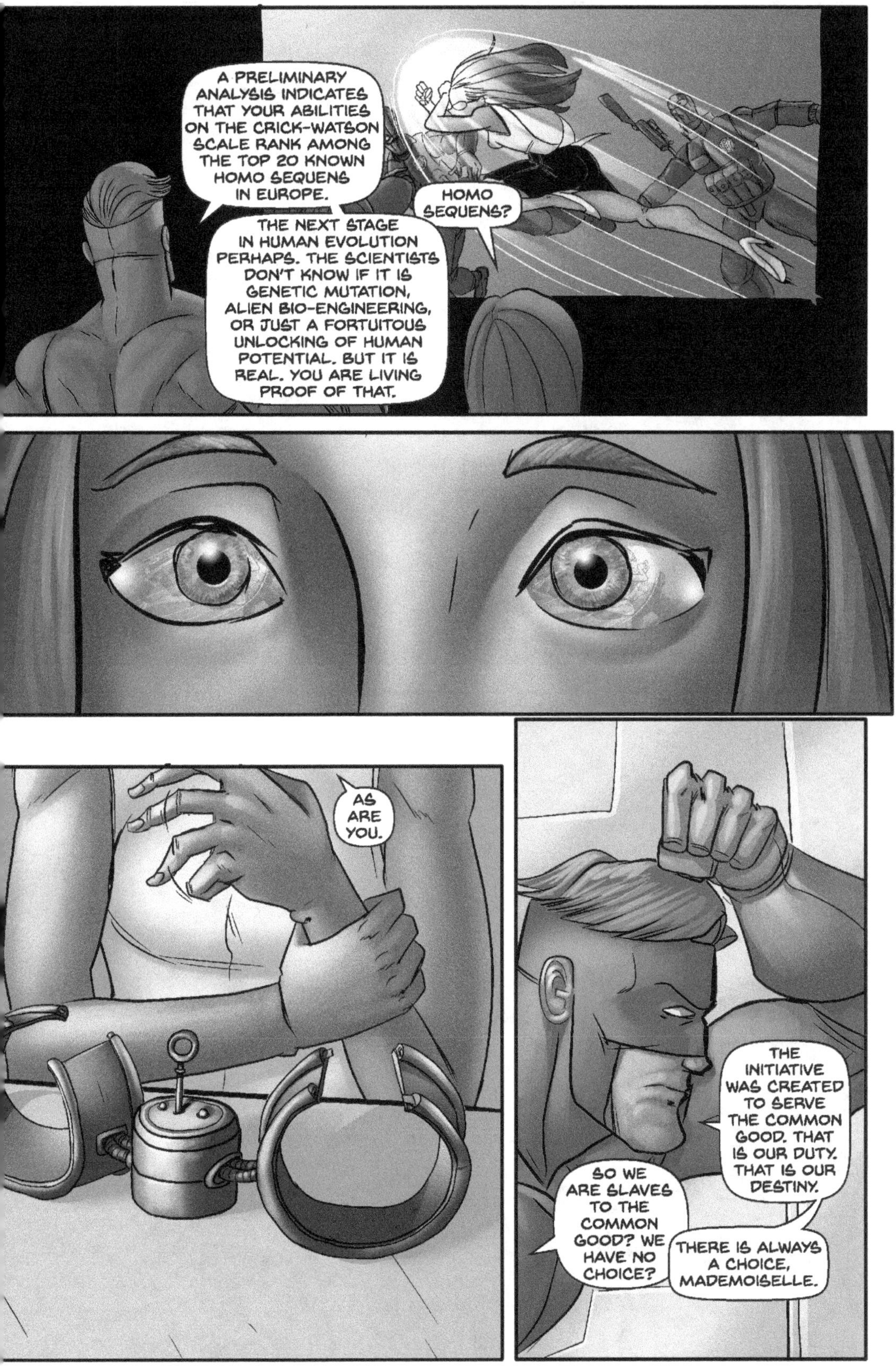
A PRELIMINARY ANALYSIS INDICATES THAT YOUR ABILITIES ON THE CRICK-WATSON SCALE RANK AMONG THE TOP 20 KNOWN HOMO SEQUENS IN EUROPE.
HOMO SEQUENS?
THE NEXT STAGE IN HUMAN EVOLUTION PERHAPS. THE SCIENTISTS DON'T KNOW IF IT IS GENETIC MUTATION, ALIEN BIO-ENGINEERING, OR JUST A FORTUITOUS UNLOCKING OF HUMAN POTENTIAL. BUT IT IS REAL. YOU ARE LIVING PROOF OF THAT.
AS ARE YOU.
THE INITIATIVE WAS CREATED TO SERVE THE COMMON GOOD. THAT IS OUR DUTY. THAT IS OUR DESTINY.
SO WE ARE SLAVES TO THE COMMON GOOD? WE HAVE NO CHOICE?
THERE IS ALWAYS A CHOICE, MADEMOISELLE.

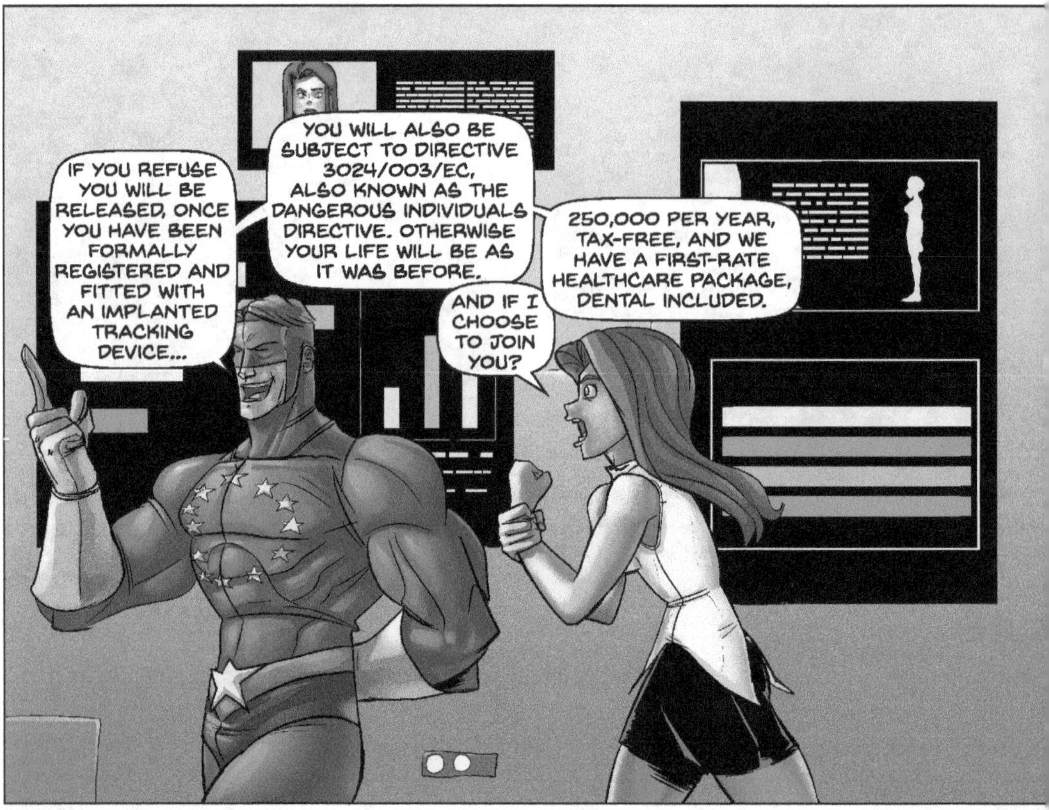
IF YOU REFUSE YOU WILL BE RELEASED, ONCE YOU HAVE BEEN FORMALLY REGISTERED AND FITTED WITH AN IMPLANTED TRACKING DEVICE...
YOU WILL ALSO BE SUBJECT TO DIRECTIVE 3024/003/EC, ALSO KNOWN AS THE DANGEROUS INDIVIDUALS DIRECTIVE. OTHERWISE YOUR LIFE WILL BE AS IT WAS BEFORE.
AND IF I CHOOSE TO JOIN YOU?
250,000 PER YEAR, TAX-FREE, AND WE HAVE A FIRST-RATE HEALTHCARE PACKAGE, DENTAL INCLUDED.

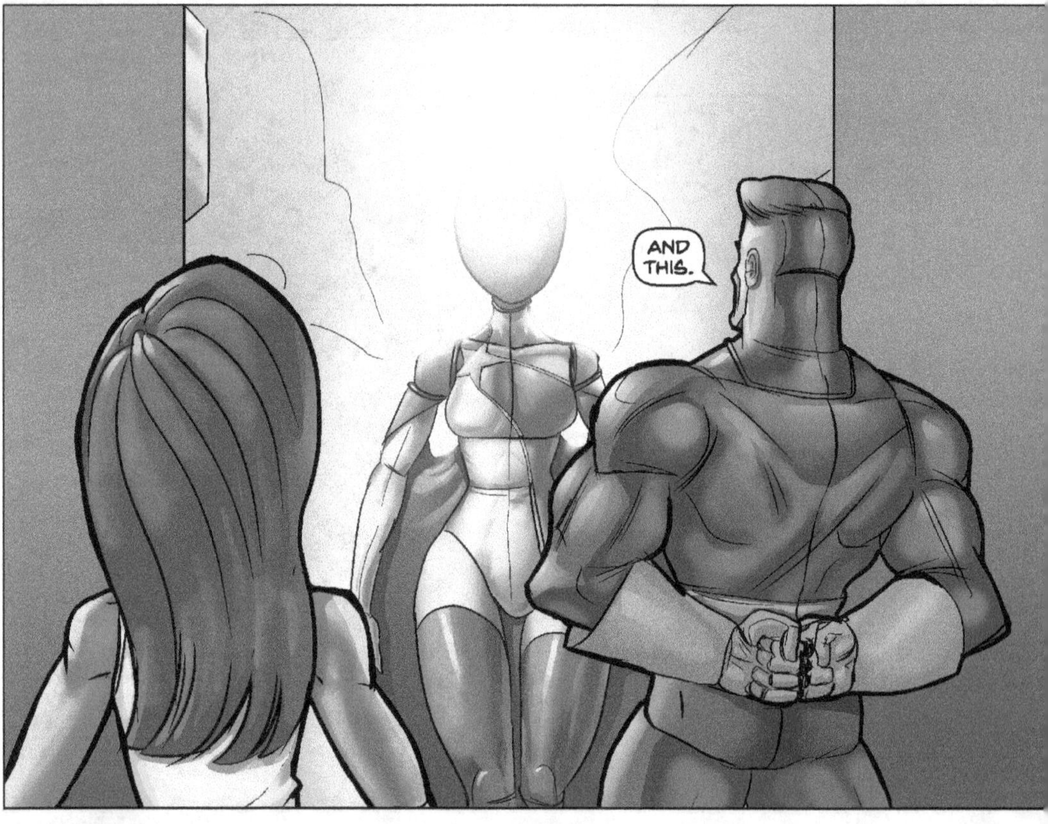
AND THIS.

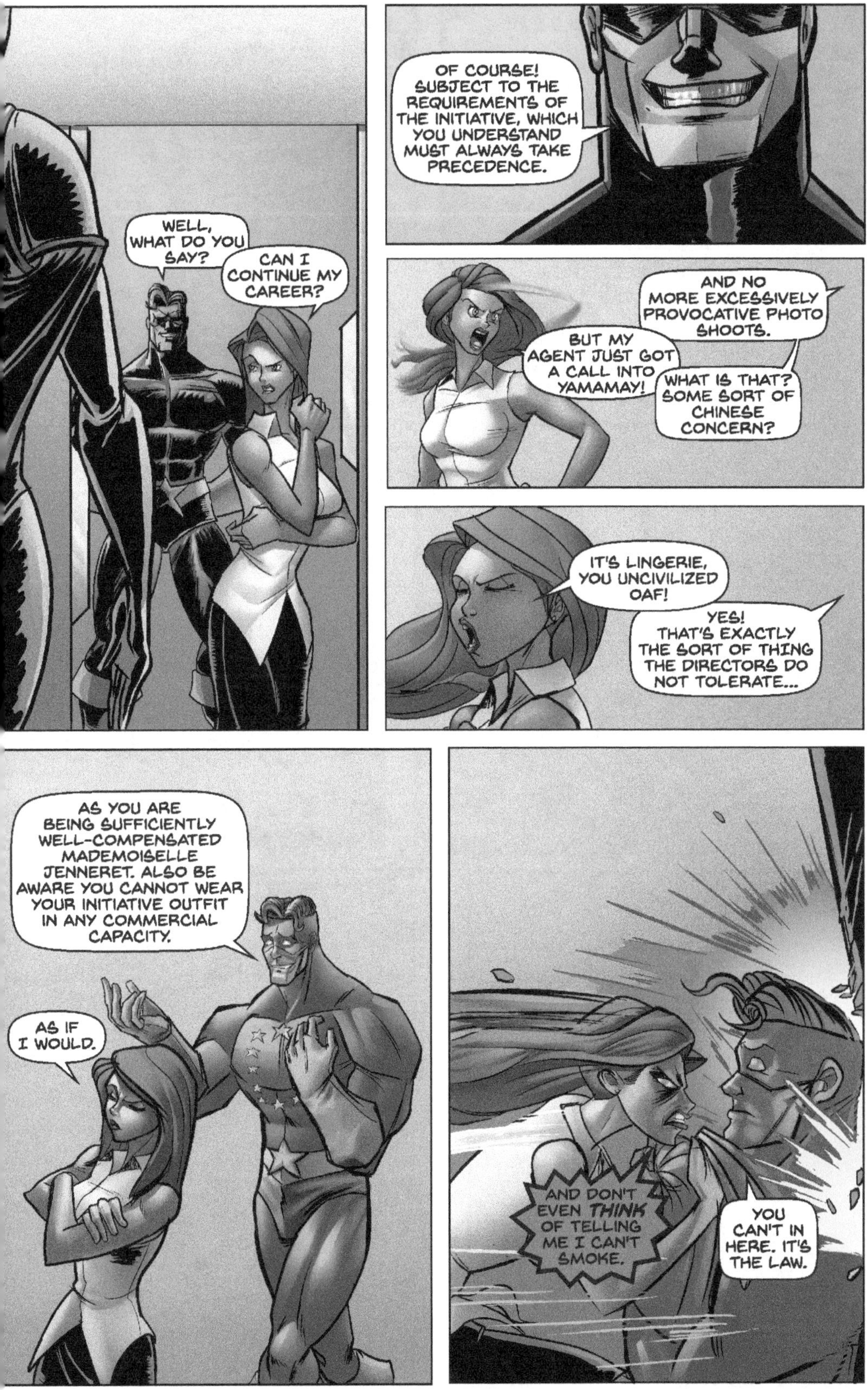
WELL, WHAT DO YOU SAY?
CAN I CONTINUE MY CAREER?
OF COURSE! SUBJECT TO THE REQUIREMENTS OF THE INITIATIVE, WHICH YOU UNDERSTAND MUST ALWAYS TAKE PRECEDENCE.
AND NO MORE EXCESSIVELY PROVOCATIVE PHOTO SHOOTS.
BUT MY AGENT JUST GOT A CALL INTO YAMAMAY!
WHAT IS THAT? SOME SORT OF CHINESE CONCERN?
IT'S LINGERIE, YOU UNCIVILIZED OAF!
YES! THAT'S EXACTLY THE SORT OF THING THE DIRECTORS DO NOT TOLERATE...
AS YOU ARE BEING SUFFICIENTLY WELL-COMPENSATED MADEMOISELLE JENNERET. ALSO BE AWARE YOU CANNOT WEAR YOUR INITIATIVE OUTFIT IN ANY COMMERCIAL CAPACITY.
AS IF I WOULD.
AND DON'T EVEN THINK OF TELLING ME I CAN'T SMOKE.
YOU CAN'T IN HERE. IT'S THE LAW.

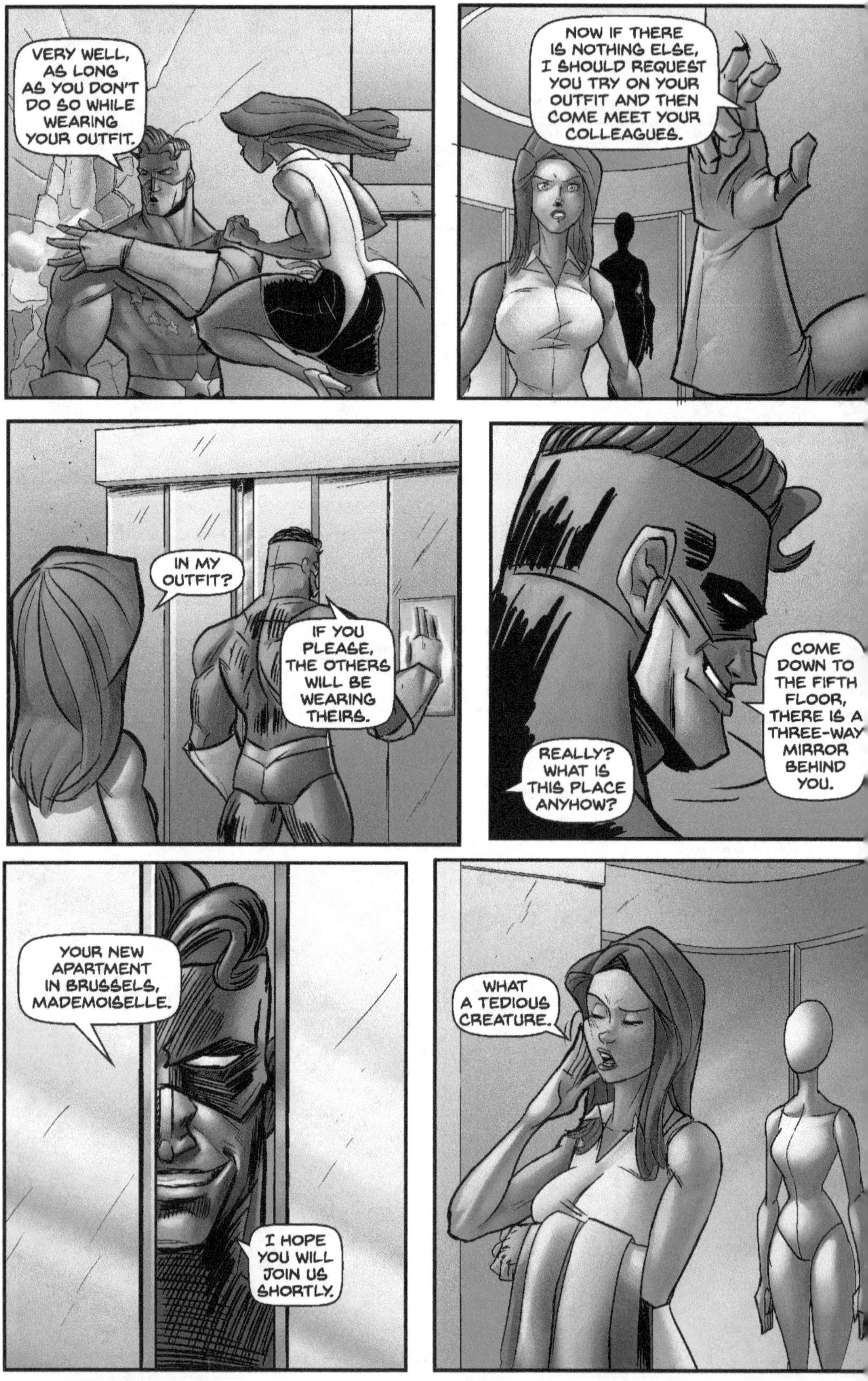
VERY WELL, AS LONG AS YOU DON'T DO SO WHILE WEARING YOUR OUTFIT.
NOW IF THERE IS NOTHING ELSE, I SHOULD REQUEST YOU TRY ON YOUR OUTFIT AND THEN COME MEET YOUR COLLEAGUES.
IN MY OUTFIT?
IF YOU PLEASE, THE OTHERS WILL BE WEARING THEIRS.
COME DOWN TO THE FIFTH FLOOR, THERE IS A THREE-WAY MIRROR BEHIND YOU.
REALLY? WHAT IS THIS PLACE ANYHOW?
YOUR NEW APARTMENT IN BRUSSELS, MADEMOISELLE.
I HOPE YOU WILL JOIN US SHORTLY.
WHAT A TEDIOUS CREATURE.

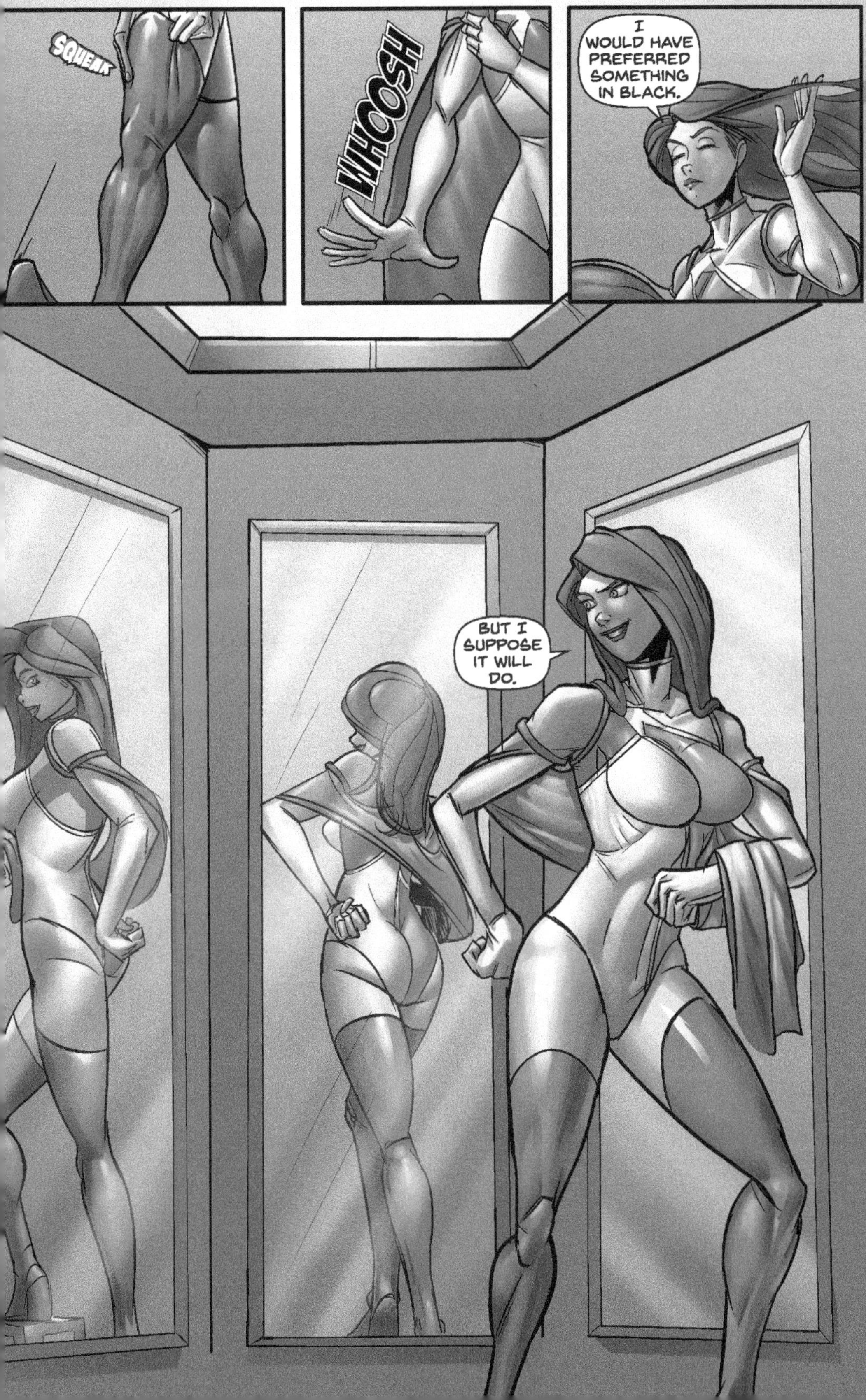
SQUEAK
WHOOSH
I WOULD HAVE PREFERRED SOMETHING IN BLACK.
BUT I SUPPOSE IT WILL DO.

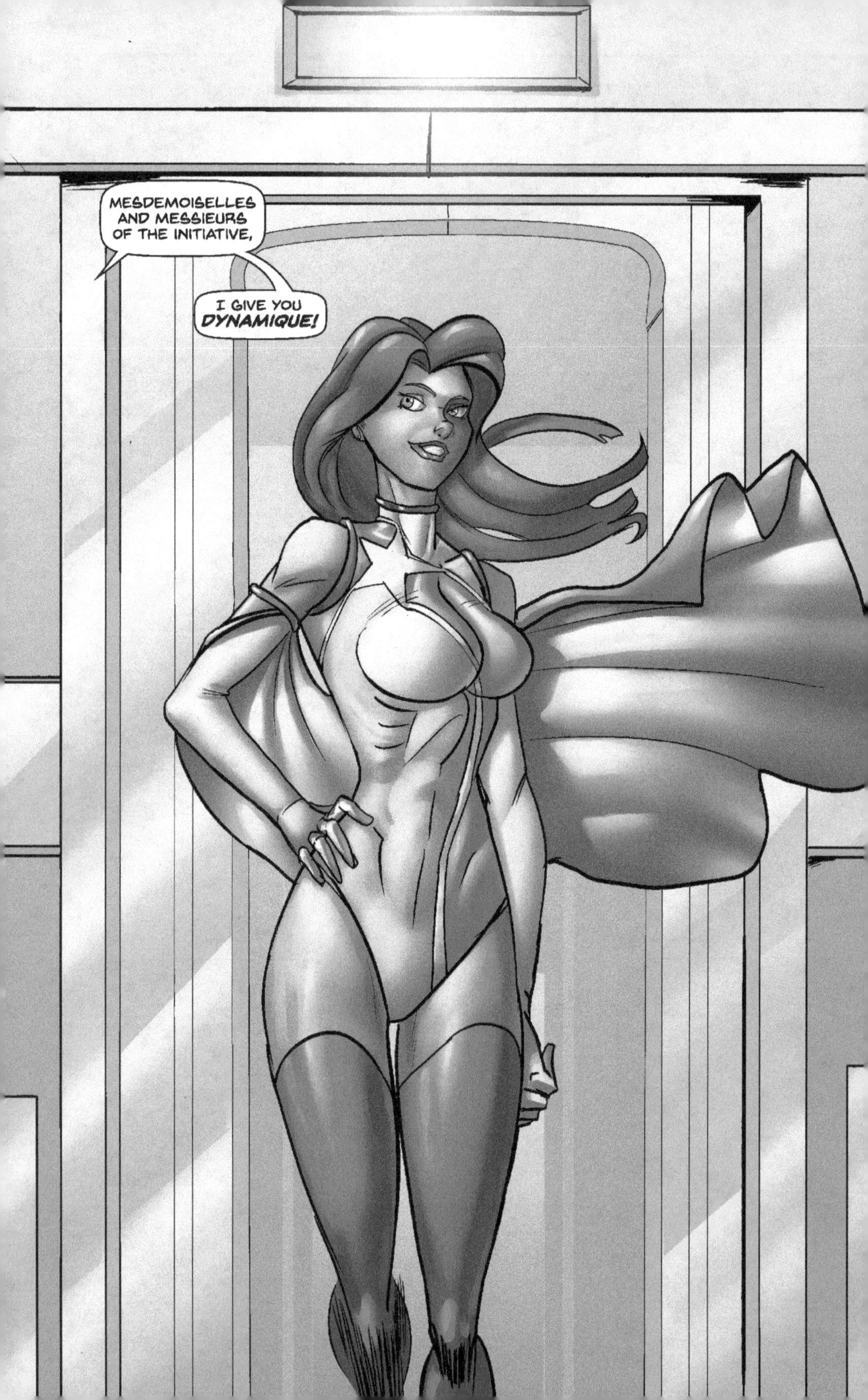
MESDEMOISELLES AND MESSIEURS OF THE INITIATIVE,
I GIVE YOU *DYNAMIQUE!*

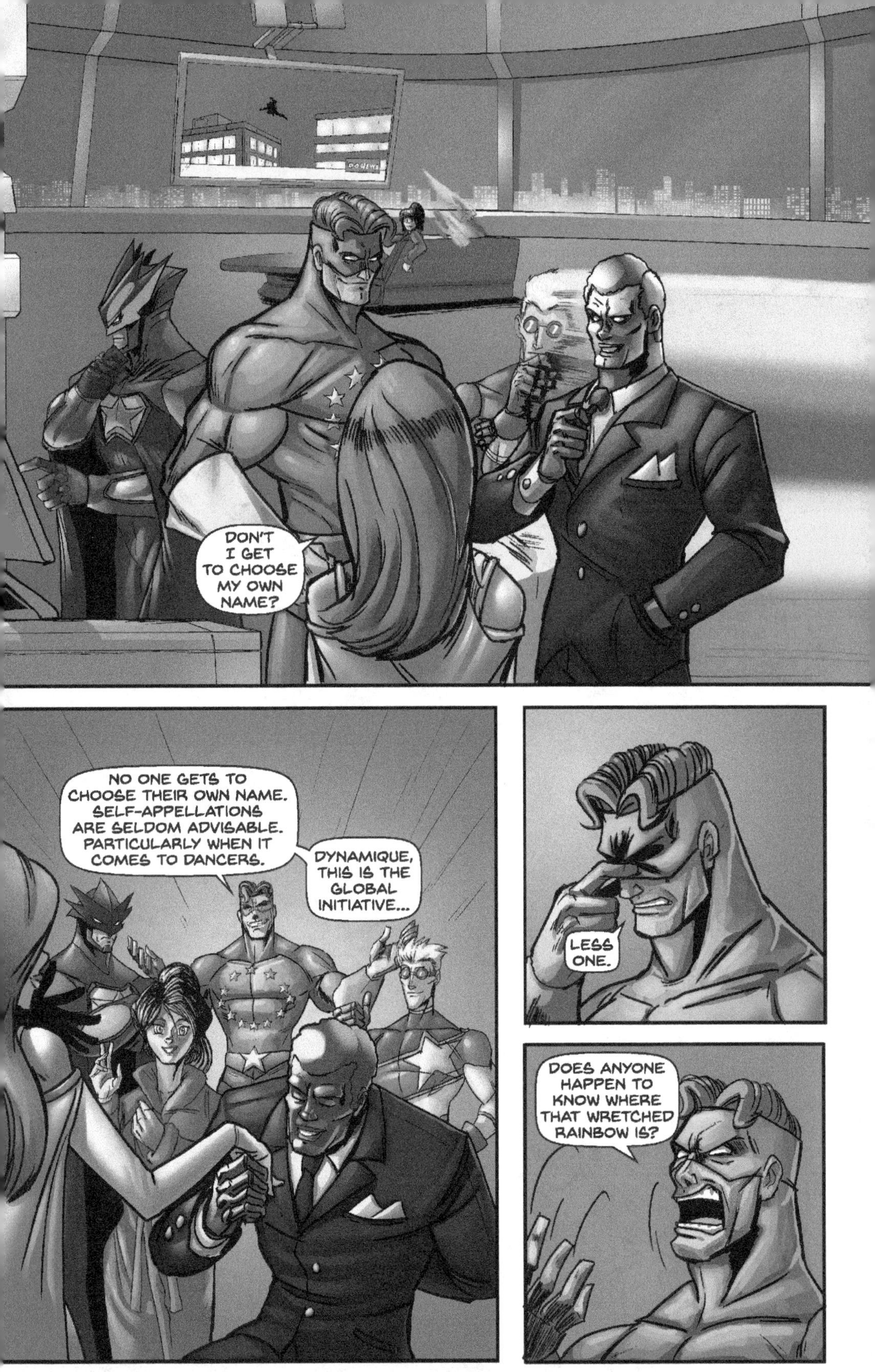
DON'T I GET TO CHOOSE MY OWN NAME?
NO ONE GETS TO CHOOSE THEIR OWN NAME. SELF-APPELLATIONS ARE SELDOM ADVISABLE. PARTICULARLY WHEN IT COMES TO DANCERS.
DYNAMIQUE, THIS IS THE GLOBAL INITIATIVE...
LESS ONE.
DOES ANYONE HAPPEN TO KNOW WHERE THAT WRETCHED RAINBOW IS?

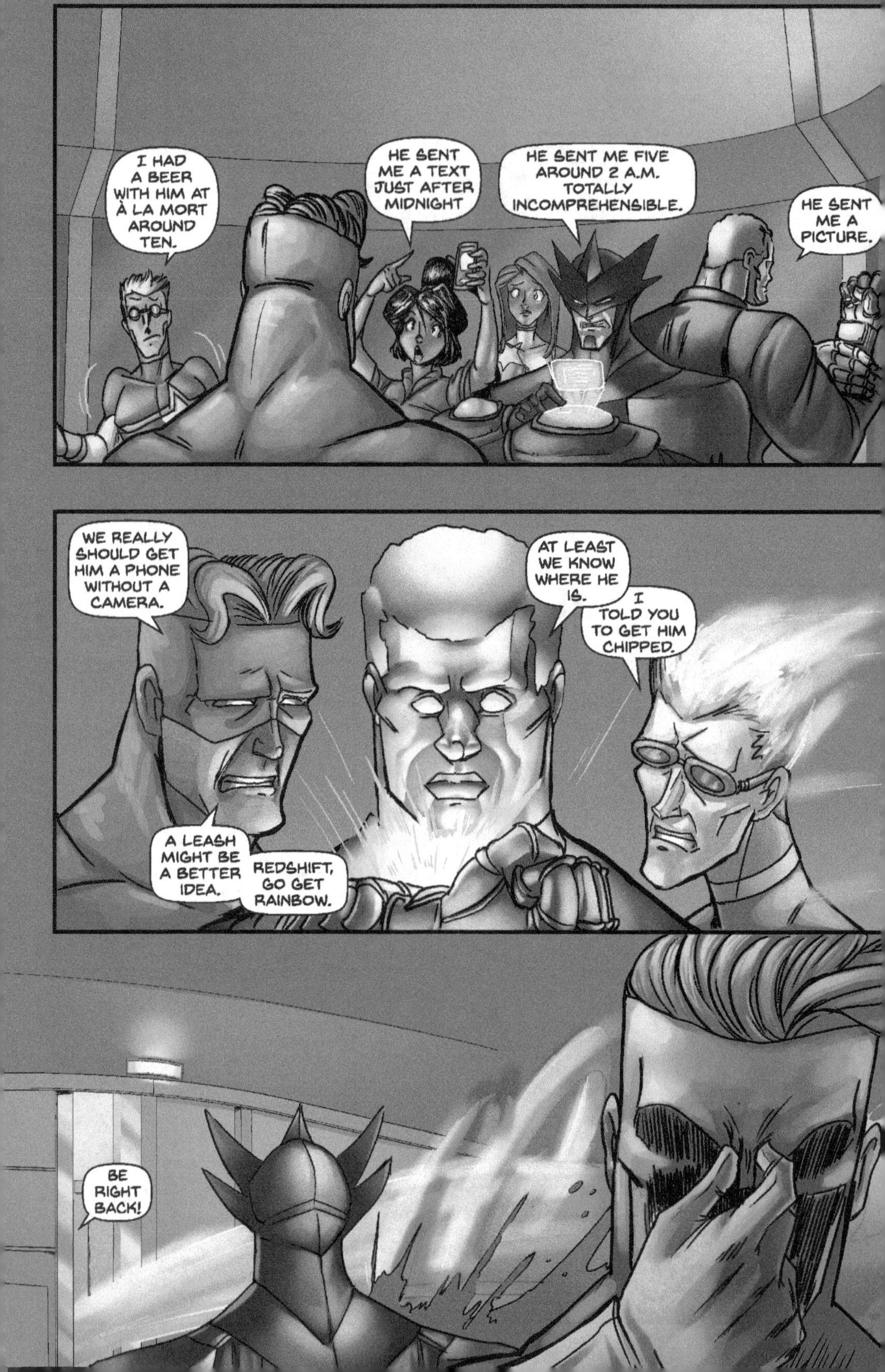
I HAD A BEER WITH HIM AT À LA MORT AROUND TEN.
HE SENT ME A TEXT JUST AFTER MIDNIGHT
HE SENT ME FIVE AROUND 2 A.M. TOTALLY INCOMPREHENSIBLE.
HE SENT ME A PICTURE.
WE REALLY SHOULD GET HIM A PHONE WITHOUT A CAMERA.
AT LEAST WE KNOW WHERE HE IS.
I TOLD YOU TO GET HIM CHIPPED.
A LEASH MIGHT BE A BETTER IDEA.
REDSHIFT, GO GET RAINBOW.
BE RIGHT BACK!

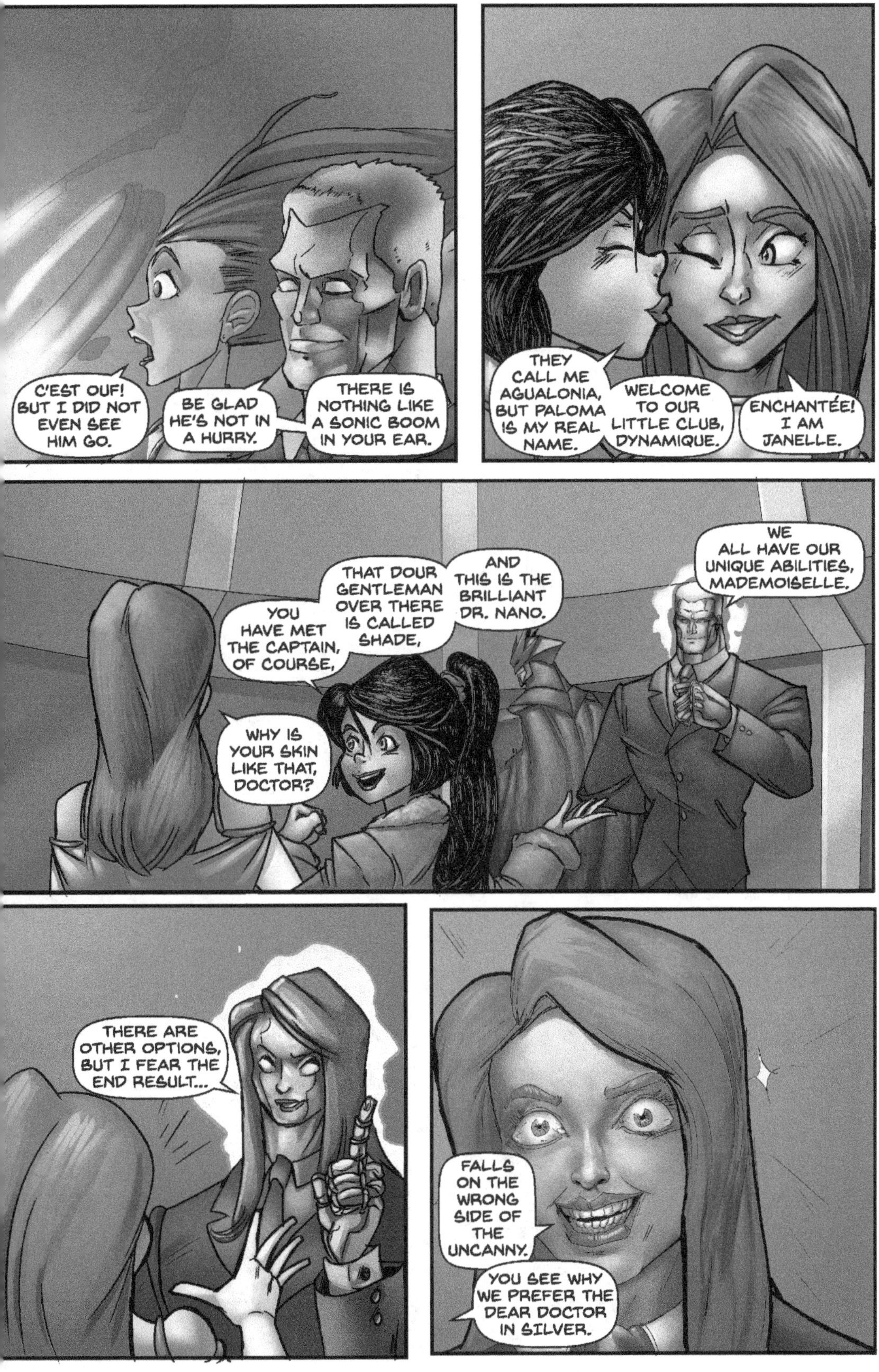
C'EST OUF! BUT I DID NOT EVEN SEE HIM GO.
BE GLAD HE'S NOT IN A HURRY.
THERE IS NOTHING LIKE A SONIC BOOM IN YOUR EAR.
THEY CALL ME AGUALONIA, BUT PALOMA IS MY REAL NAME.
WELCOME TO OUR LITTLE CLUB, DYNAMIQUE.
ENCHANTÉE! I AM JANELLE.
YOU HAVE MET THE CAPTAIN, OF COURSE,
THAT DOUR GENTLEMAN OVER THERE IS CALLED SHADE,
AND THIS IS THE BRILLIANT DR. NANO.
WE ALL HAVE OUR UNIQUE ABILITIES, MADEMOISELLE.
WHY IS YOUR SKIN LIKE THAT, DOCTOR?
THERE ARE OTHER OPTIONS, BUT I FEAR THE END RESULT...
FALLS ON THE WRONG SIDE OF THE UNCANNY.
YOU SEE WHY WE PREFER THE DEAR DOCTOR IN SILVER.

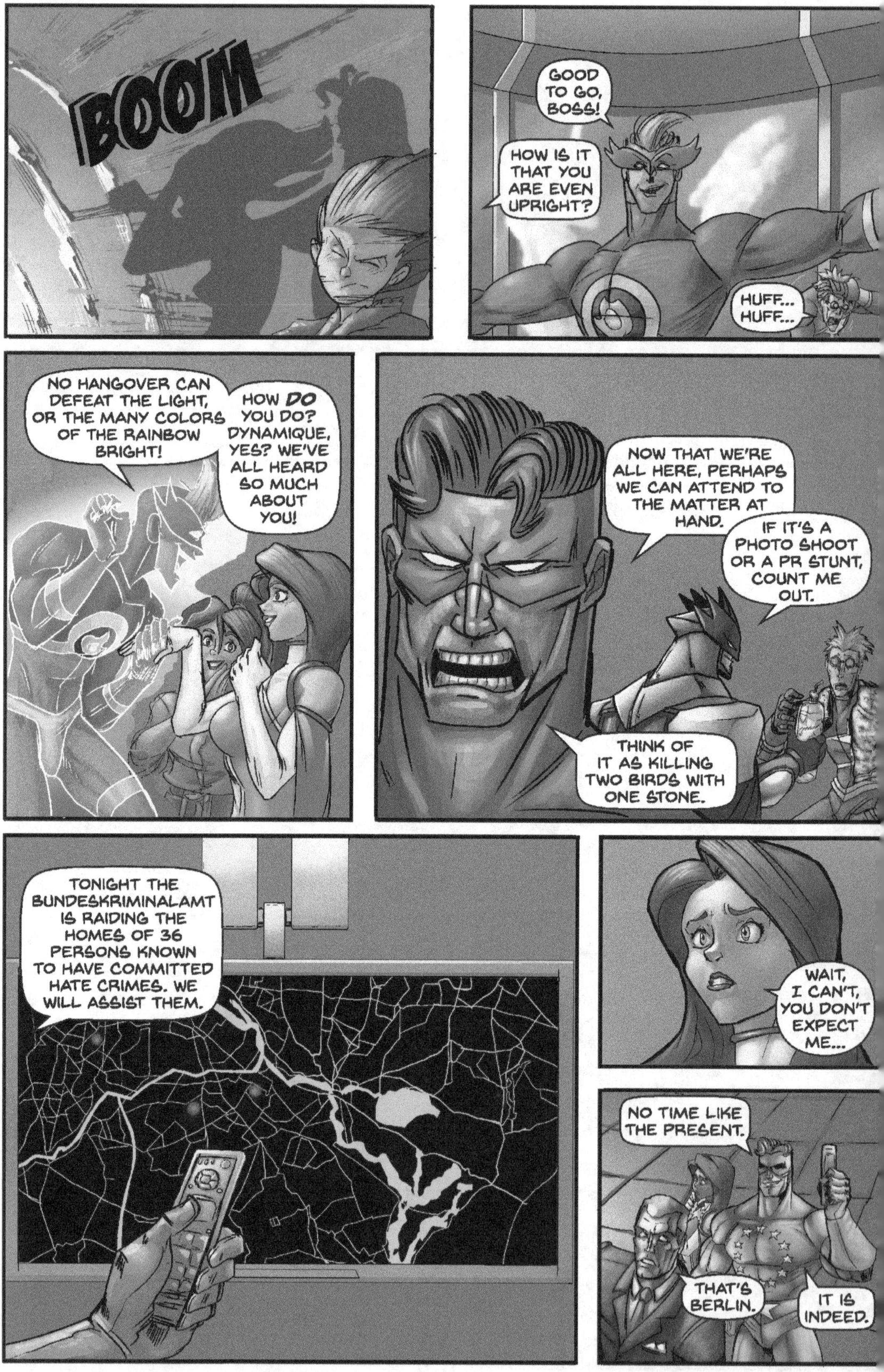
BOOM
GOOD TO GO, BOSS!
HOW IS IT THAT YOU ARE EVEN UPRIGHT?
HUFF... HUFF...
NO HANGOVER CAN DEFEAT THE LIGHT, OR THE MANY COLORS OF THE RAINBOW BRIGHT!
HOW *DO* YOU DO? DYNAMIQUE, YES? WE'VE ALL HEARD SO MUCH ABOUT YOU!
NOW THAT WE'RE ALL HERE, PERHAPS WE CAN ATTEND TO THE MATTER AT HAND.
IF IT'S A PHOTO SHOOT OR A PR STUNT, COUNT ME OUT.
THINK OF IT AS KILLING TWO BIRDS WITH ONE STONE.
TONIGHT THE BUNDESKRIMINALAMT IS RAIDING THE HOMES OF 36 PERSONS KNOWN TO HAVE COMMITTED HATE CRIMES. WE WILL ASSIST THEM.
WAIT, I CAN'T, YOU DON'T EXPECT ME...
NO TIME LIKE THE PRESENT.
THAT'S BERLIN.
IT IS INDEED.

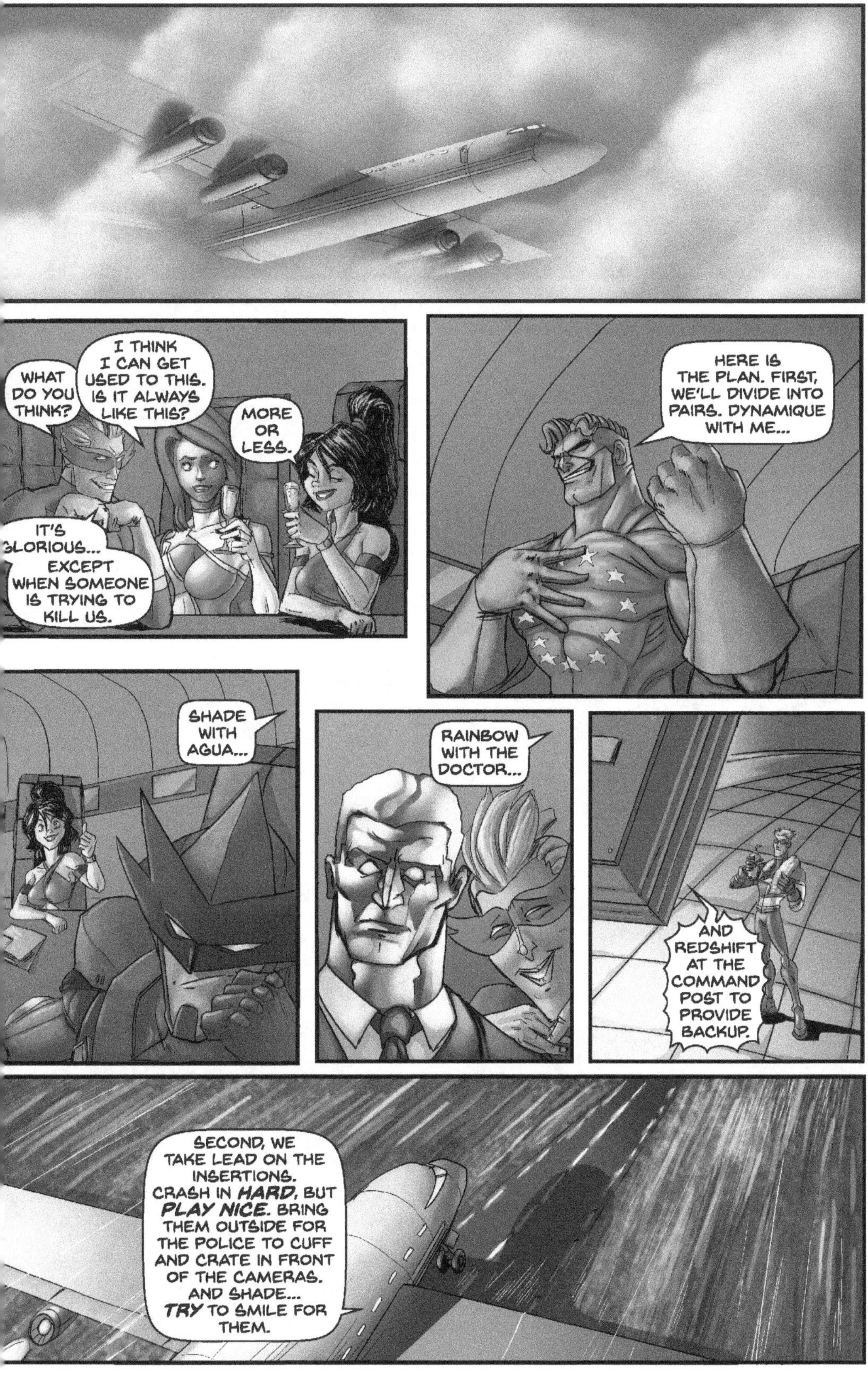
WHAT DO YOU THINK?
I THINK I CAN GET USED TO THIS. IS IT ALWAYS LIKE THIS?
MORE OR LESS.
IT'S GLORIOUS... EXCEPT WHEN SOMEONE IS TRYING TO KILL US.
HERE IS THE PLAN. FIRST, WE'LL DIVIDE INTO PAIRS. DYNAMIQUE WITH ME...
SHADE WITH AGUA...
RAINBOW WITH THE DOCTOR...
AND REDSHIFT AT THE COMMAND POST TO PROVIDE BACKUP.
SECOND, WE TAKE LEAD ON THE INSERTIONS. CRASH IN HARD, BUT PLAY NICE. BRING THEM OUTSIDE FOR THE POLICE TO CUFF AND CRATE IN FRONT OF THE CAMERAS. AND SHADE... TRY TO SMILE FOR THEM.

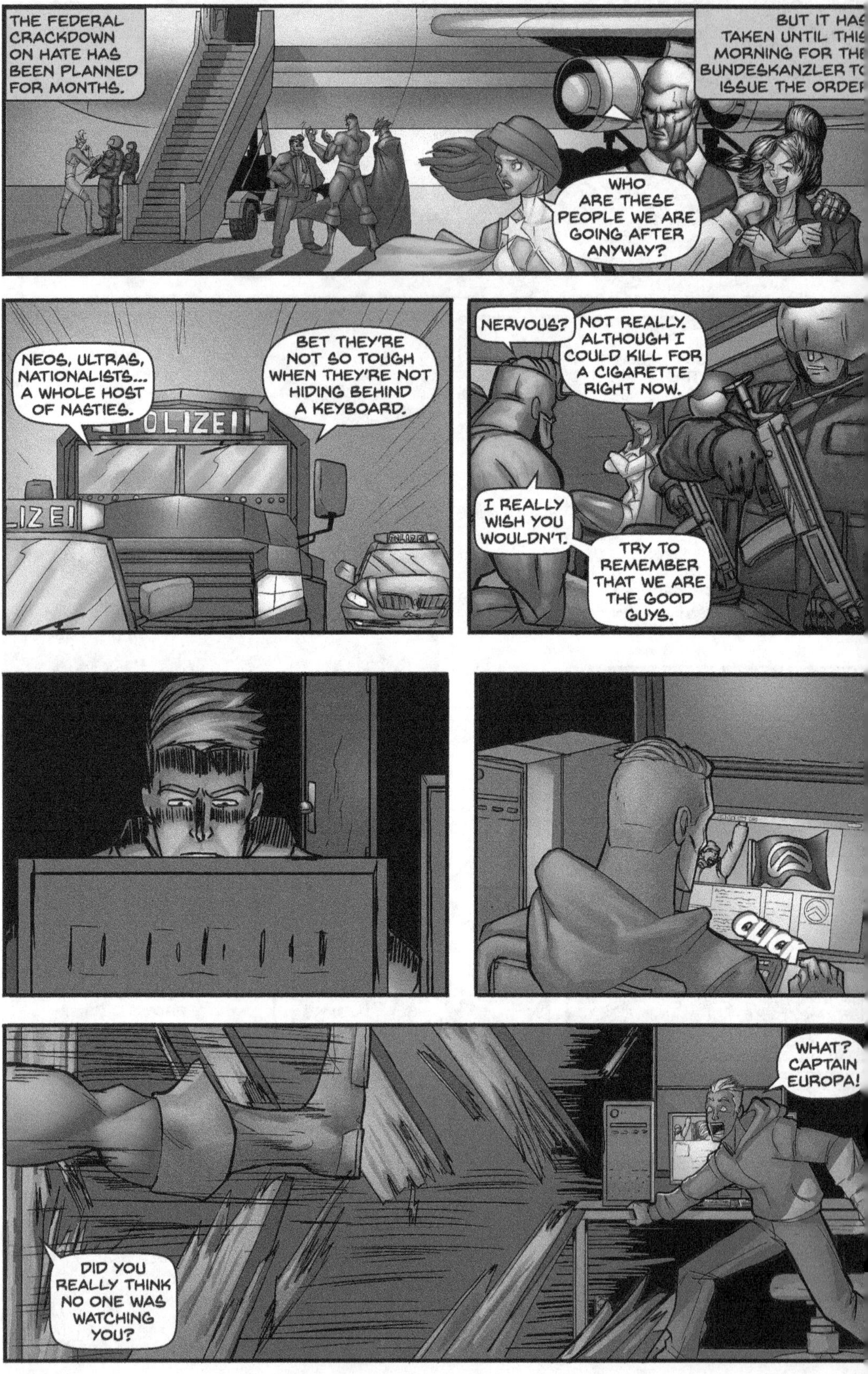
THE FEDERAL CRACKDOWN ON HATE HAS BEEN PLANNED FOR MONTHS.
BUT IT HAS TAKEN UNTIL THIS MORNING FOR THE BUNDESKANZLER TO ISSUE THE ORDER
WHO ARE THESE PEOPLE WE ARE GOING AFTER ANYWAY?
NEOS, ULTRAS, NATIONALISTS... A WHOLE HOST OF NASTIES.
BET THEY'RE NOT SO TOUGH WHEN THEY'RE NOT HIDING BEHIND A KEYBOARD.
POLIZEI
LIZEI
NERVOUS?
NOT REALLY. ALTHOUGH I COULD KILL FOR A CIGARETTE RIGHT NOW.
I REALLY WISH YOU WOULDN'T.
TRY TO REMEMBER THAT WE ARE THE GOOD GUYS.
CLICK
WHAT? CAPTAIN EUROPA!
DID YOU REALLY THINK NO ONE WAS WATCHING YOU?

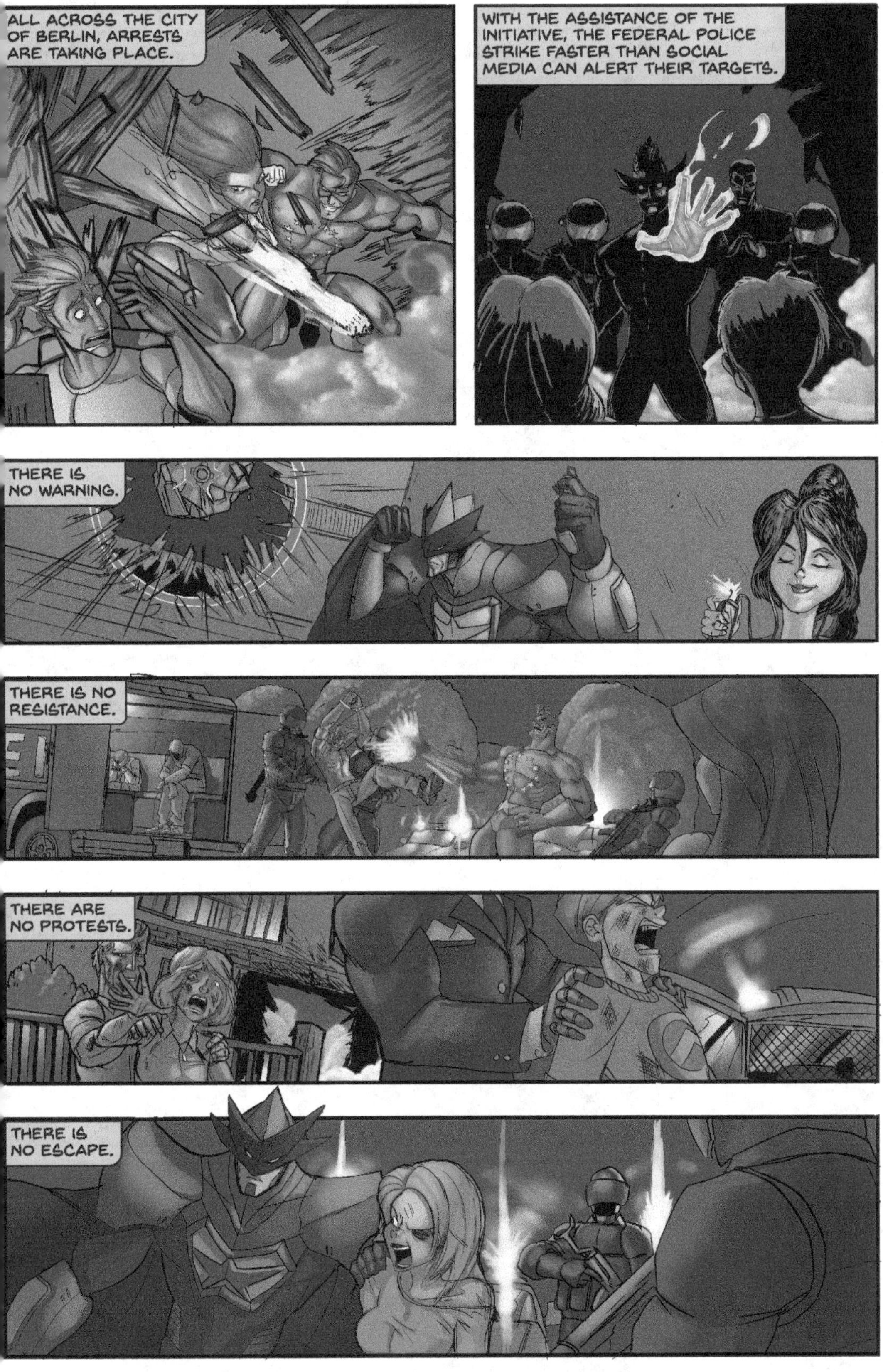
ALL ACROSS THE CITY OF BERLIN, ARRESTS ARE TAKING PLACE.
WITH THE ASSISTANCE OF THE INITIATIVE, THE FEDERAL POLICE STRIKE FASTER THAN SOCIAL MEDIA CAN ALERT THEIR TARGETS.
THERE IS NO WARNING.
THERE IS NO RESISTANCE.
THERE ARE NO PROTESTS.
THERE IS NO ESCAPE.

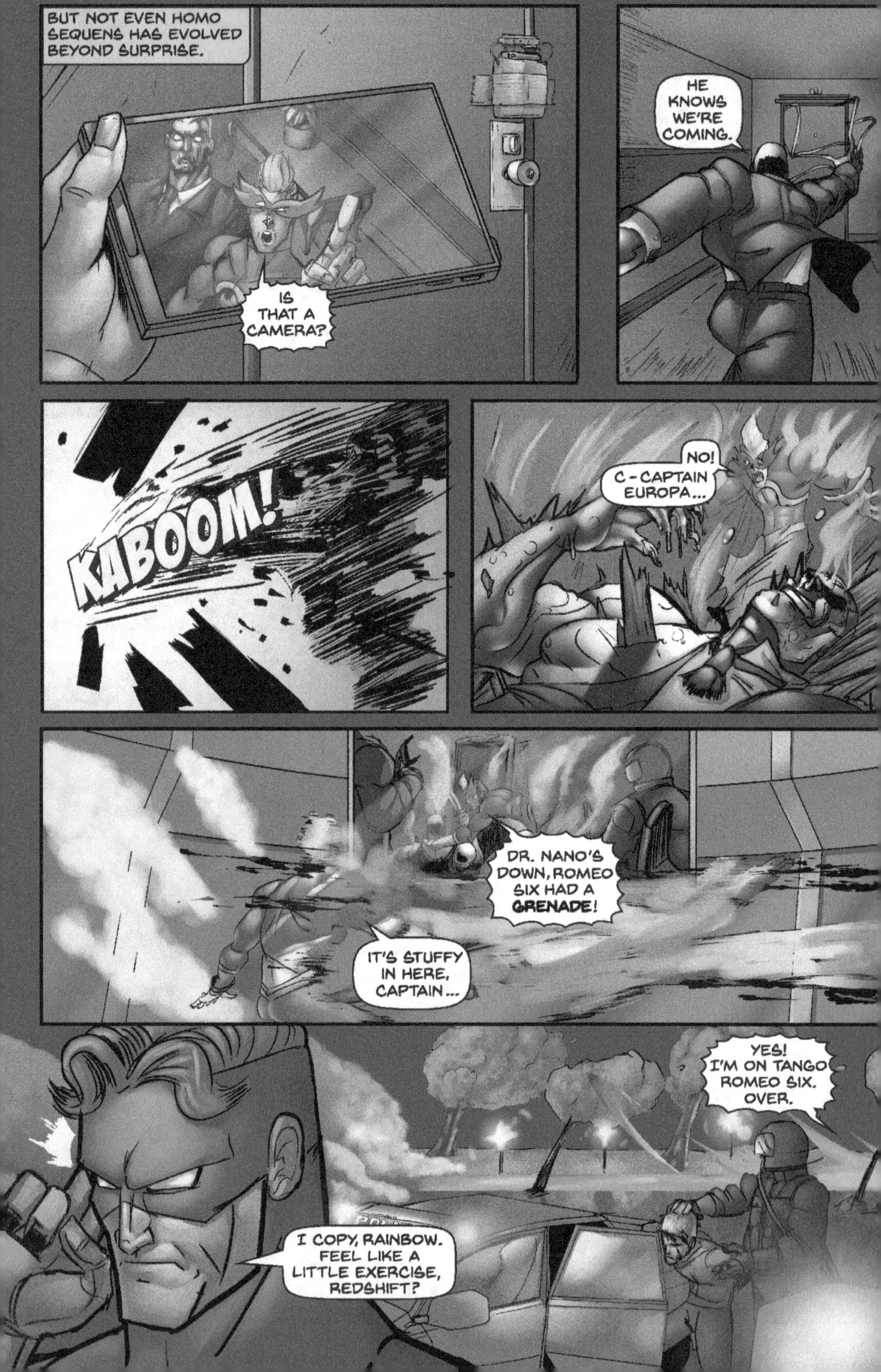
BUT NOT EVEN HOMO SEQUENS HAS EVOLVED BEYOND SURPRISE.
IS THAT A CAMERA?
HE KNOWS WE'RE COMING.
KABOOM!
NO! C-CAPTAIN EUROPA...
DR. NANO'S DOWN, ROMEO SIX HAD A **GRENADE**!
IT'S STUFFY IN HERE, CAPTAIN...
YES! I'M ON TANGO ROMEO SIX. OVER.
I COPY, RAINBOW. FEEL LIKE A LITTLE EXERCISE, REDSHIFT?

FEAR INSPIRES A MAN LIKE A DOG INSPIRES A RABBIT.

BUT THERE IS NO AMOUNT OF FEAR THAT CAN INSPIRE A MAN TO OUTRUN REDSHIFT.

A 90-KILOGRAM OBJECT WITH AN ACCELERATION OF 3,825 KILOMETERS PER HOUR STRIKES WITH THE FORCE OF 10 TONS.

FORTUNATELY, FOR THE FUGITIVE,

REDSHIFT SLOWS DOWN CONSIDERABLY BEFORE HITTING HIM FROM BEHIND.

CAPTAIN EUROPA, THIS IS REDSHIFT. TANGO DOWN. OVER.

COPY THAT, RED, VERY GOOD! SIT TIGHT,

WE'LL COME TO YOU. OVER.

CONGRATULATIONS, HERR RHEINHARDT. YOU GRADUATED FROM HATEPOSTING TO ATTEMPTED MURDER. WHERE DID YOU GET AN M-75 ANYWAY?

I'M NOT TELLING YOU EUROFASCISTS ANYTHING!

SO THE NAZI PUNK THINKS WE'RE THE FASCISTS?

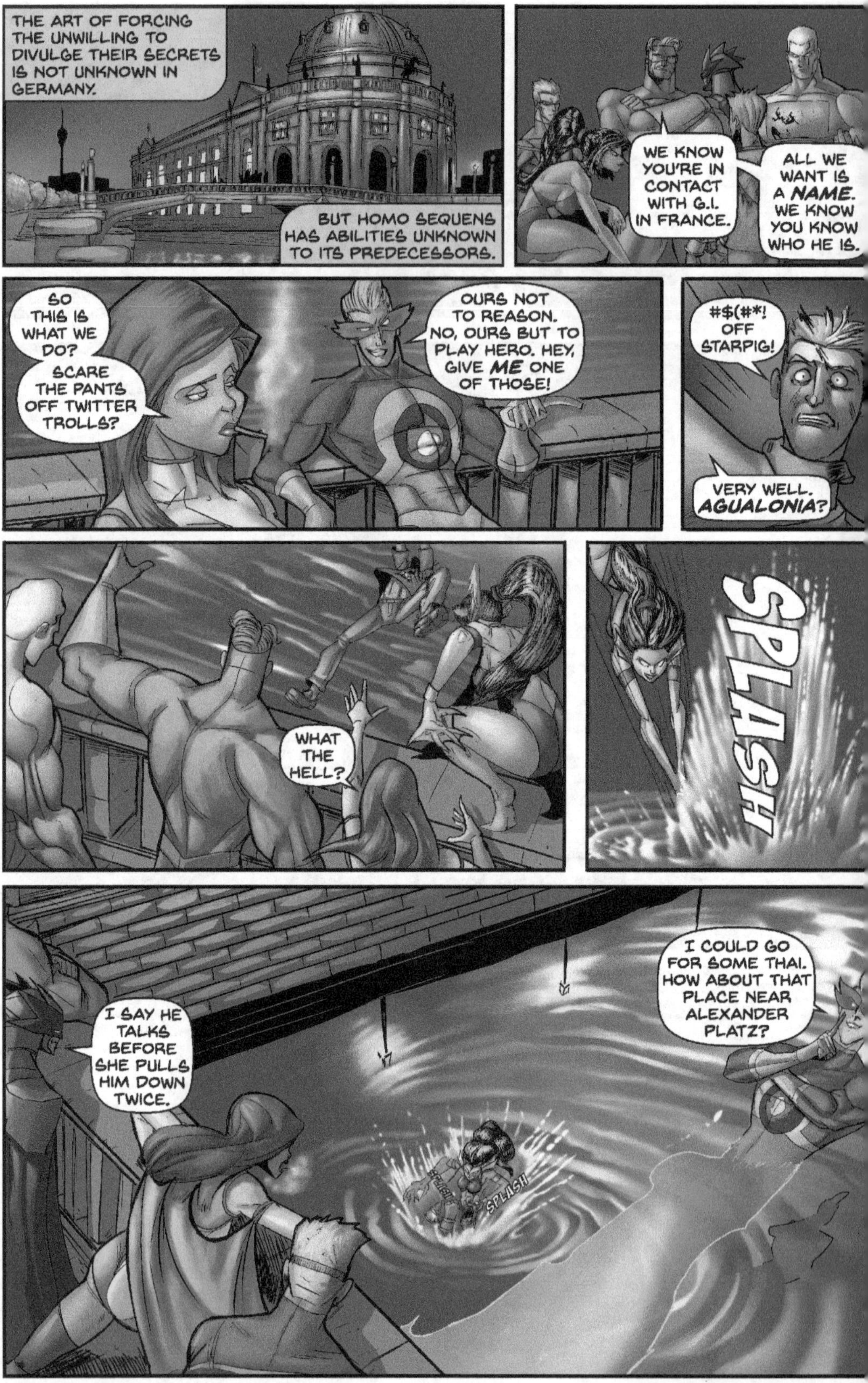
THE ART OF FORCING THE UNWILLING TO DIVULGE THEIR SECRETS IS NOT UNKNOWN IN GERMANY.
BUT HOMO SEQUENS HAS ABILITIES UNKNOWN TO ITS PREDECESSORS.
WE KNOW YOU'RE IN CONTACT WITH G.I. IN FRANCE.
ALL WE WANT IS A NAME. WE KNOW YOU KNOW WHO HE IS.
SO THIS IS WHAT WE DO?
SCARE THE PANTS OFF TWITTER TROLLS?
OURS NOT TO REASON. NO, OURS BUT TO PLAY HERO. HEY, GIVE ME ONE OF THOSE!
#$(#*! OFF STARPIG!
VERY WELL. AGUALONIA?
WHAT THE HELL?
SPLASH
I SAY HE TALKS BEFORE SHE PULLS HIM DOWN TWICE.
I COULD GO FOR SOME THAI. HOW ABOUT THAT PLACE NEAR ALEXANDER PLATZ?
SPLASH
SPLASH

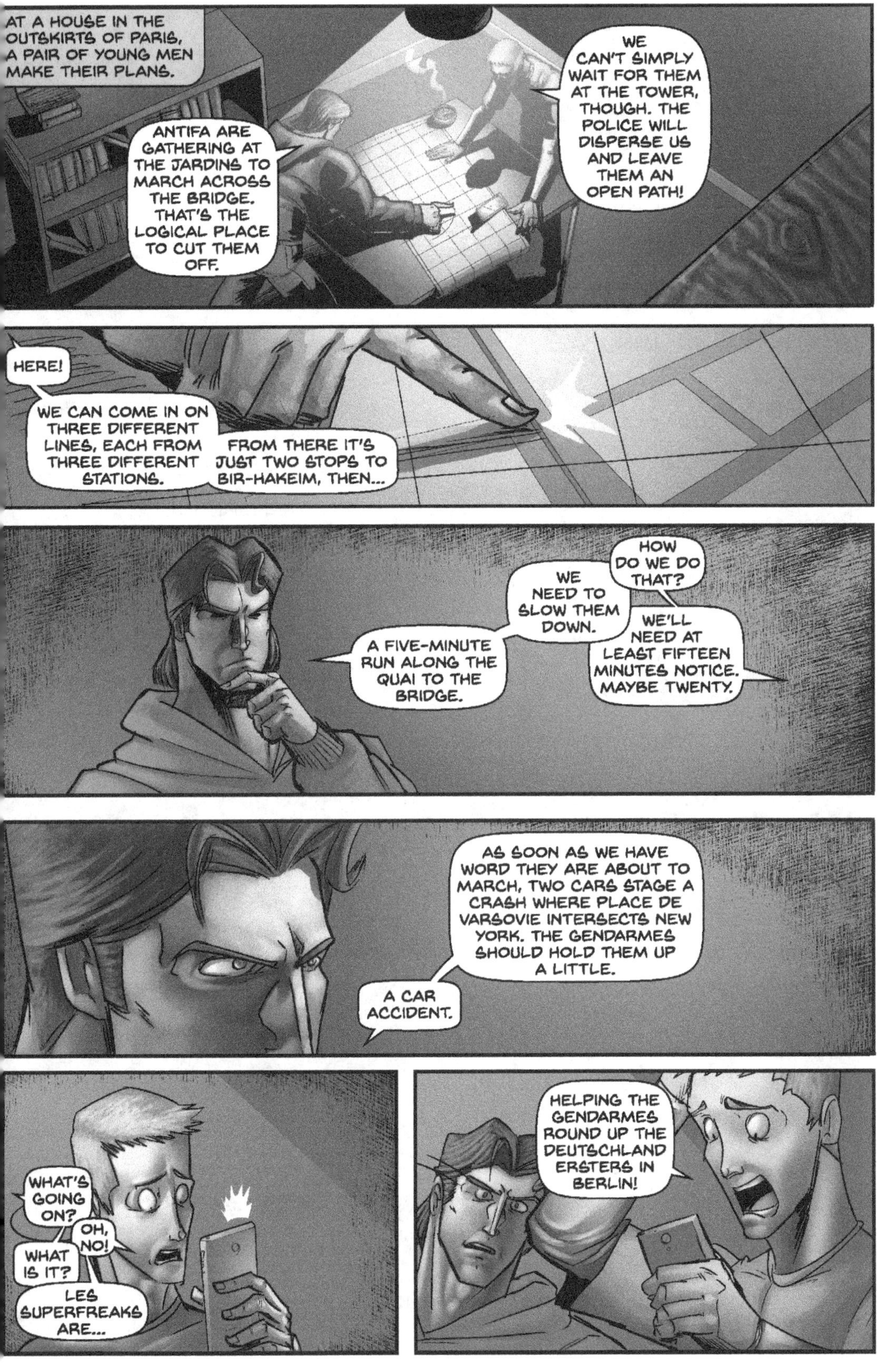
AT A HOUSE IN THE OUTSKIRTS OF PARIS, A PAIR OF YOUNG MEN MAKE THEIR PLANS.
ANTIFA ARE GATHERING AT THE JARDINS TO MARCH ACROSS THE BRIDGE. THAT'S THE LOGICAL PLACE TO CUT THEM OFF.
WE CAN'T SIMPLY WAIT FOR THEM AT THE TOWER, THOUGH. THE POLICE WILL DISPERSE US AND LEAVE THEM AN OPEN PATH!
HERE!
WE CAN COME IN ON THREE DIFFERENT LINES, EACH FROM THREE DIFFERENT STATIONS.
FROM THERE IT'S JUST TWO STOPS TO BIR-HAKEIM, THEN...
A FIVE-MINUTE RUN ALONG THE QUAI TO THE BRIDGE.
WE NEED TO SLOW THEM DOWN.
HOW DO WE DO THAT?
WE'LL NEED AT LEAST FIFTEEN MINUTES NOTICE. MAYBE TWENTY.
AS SOON AS WE HAVE WORD THEY ARE ABOUT TO MARCH, TWO CARS STAGE A CRASH WHERE PLACE DE VARSOVIE INTERSECTS NEW YORK. THE GENDARMES SHOULD HOLD THEM UP A LITTLE.
A CAR ACCIDENT.
WHAT'S GOING ON?
OH, NO!
WHAT IS IT?
LES SUPERFREAKS ARE...
HELPING THE GENDARMES ROUND UP THE DEUTSCHLAND ERSTERS IN BERLIN!

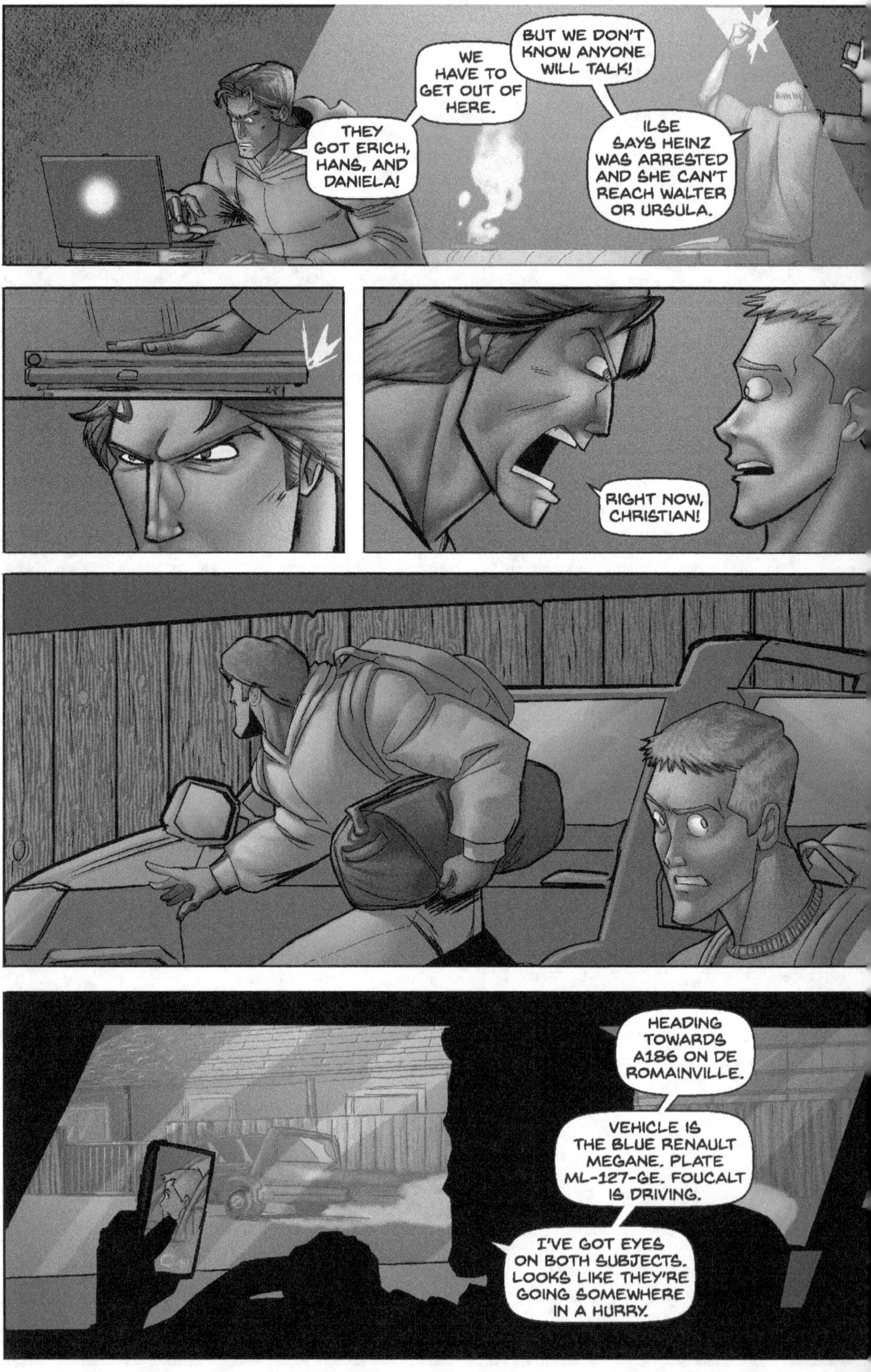
THEY GOT ERICH, HANS, AND DANIELA!
WE HAVE TO GET OUT OF HERE.
BUT WE DON'T KNOW ANYONE WILL TALK!
ILSE SAYS HEINZ WAS ARRESTED AND SHE CAN'T REACH WALTER OR URSULA.
RIGHT NOW, CHRISTIAN!
HEADING TOWARDS A186 ON DE ROMAINVILLE.
VEHICLE IS THE BLUE RENAULT MEGANE. PLATE ML-127-GE. FOUCALT IS DRIVING.
I'VE GOT EYES ON BOTH SUBJECTS. LOOKS LIKE THEY'RE GOING SOMEWHERE IN A HURRY.

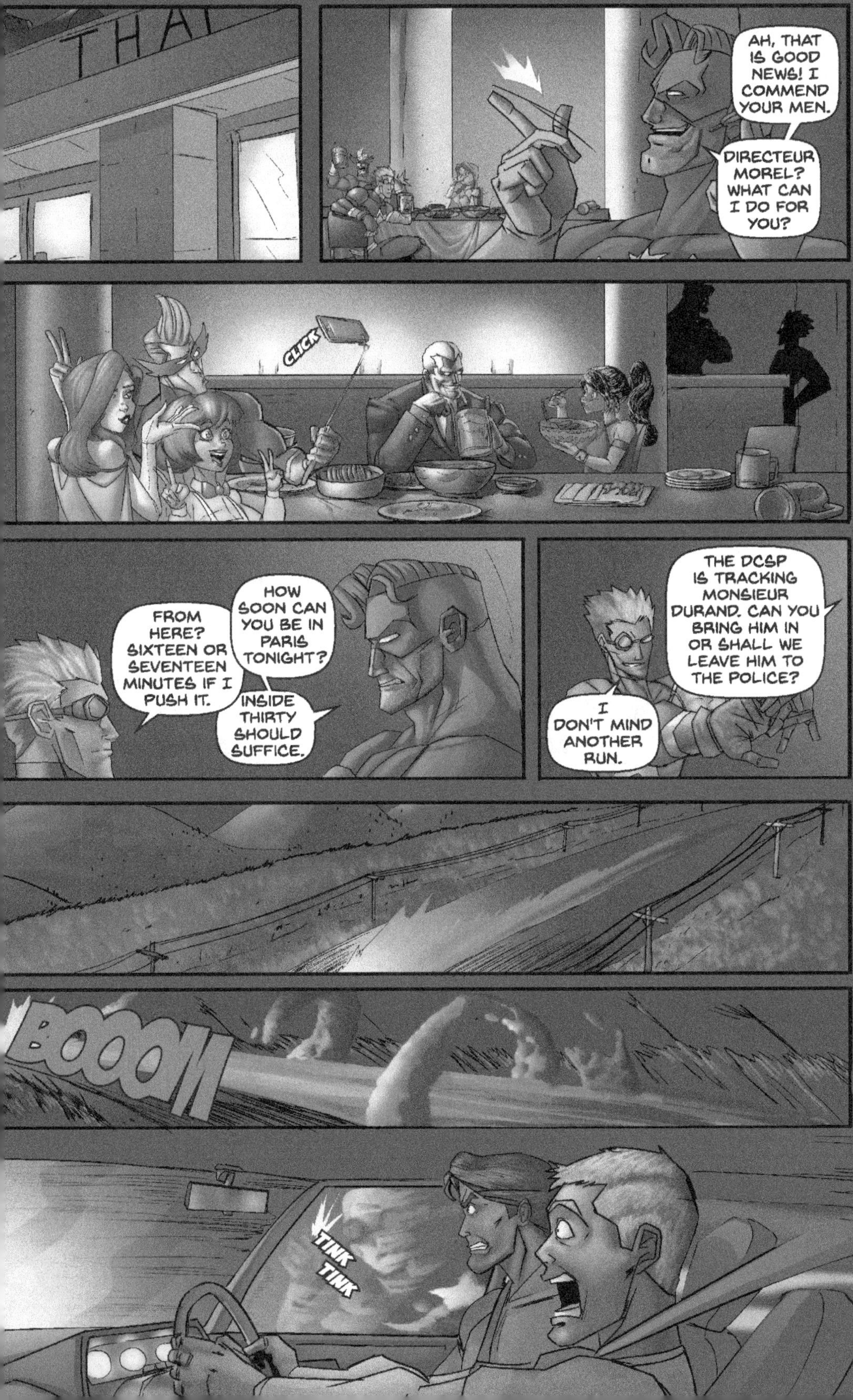
AH, THAT IS GOOD NEWS! I COMMEND YOUR MEN.
DIRECTEUR MOREL? WHAT CAN I DO FOR YOU?
CLICK
HOW SOON CAN YOU BE IN PARIS TONIGHT?
FROM HERE? SIXTEEN OR SEVENTEEN MINUTES IF I PUSH IT.
INSIDE THIRTY SHOULD SUFFICE.
THE DCSP IS TRACKING MONSIEUR DURAND. CAN YOU BRING HIM IN OR SHALL WE LEAVE HIM TO THE POLICE?
I DON'T MIND ANOTHER RUN.
BOOOM
TINK
TINK

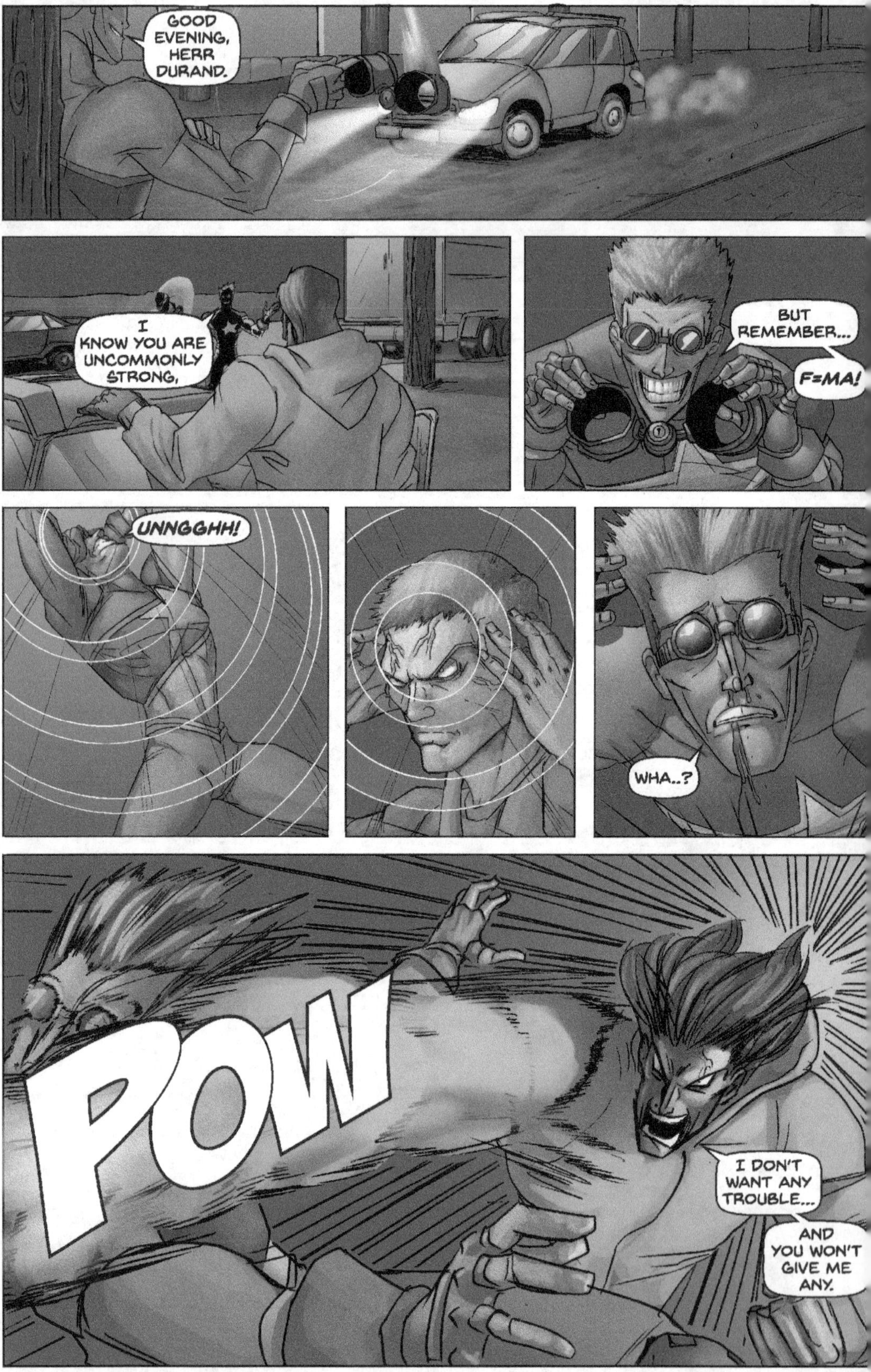
GOOD EVENING, HERR DURAND.
I KNOW YOU ARE UNCOMMONLY STRONG,
BUT REMEMBER...
F=MA!
UNNGGHH!
WHA..?
POW
I DON'T WANT ANY TROUBLE...
AND YOU WON'T GIVE ME ANY.

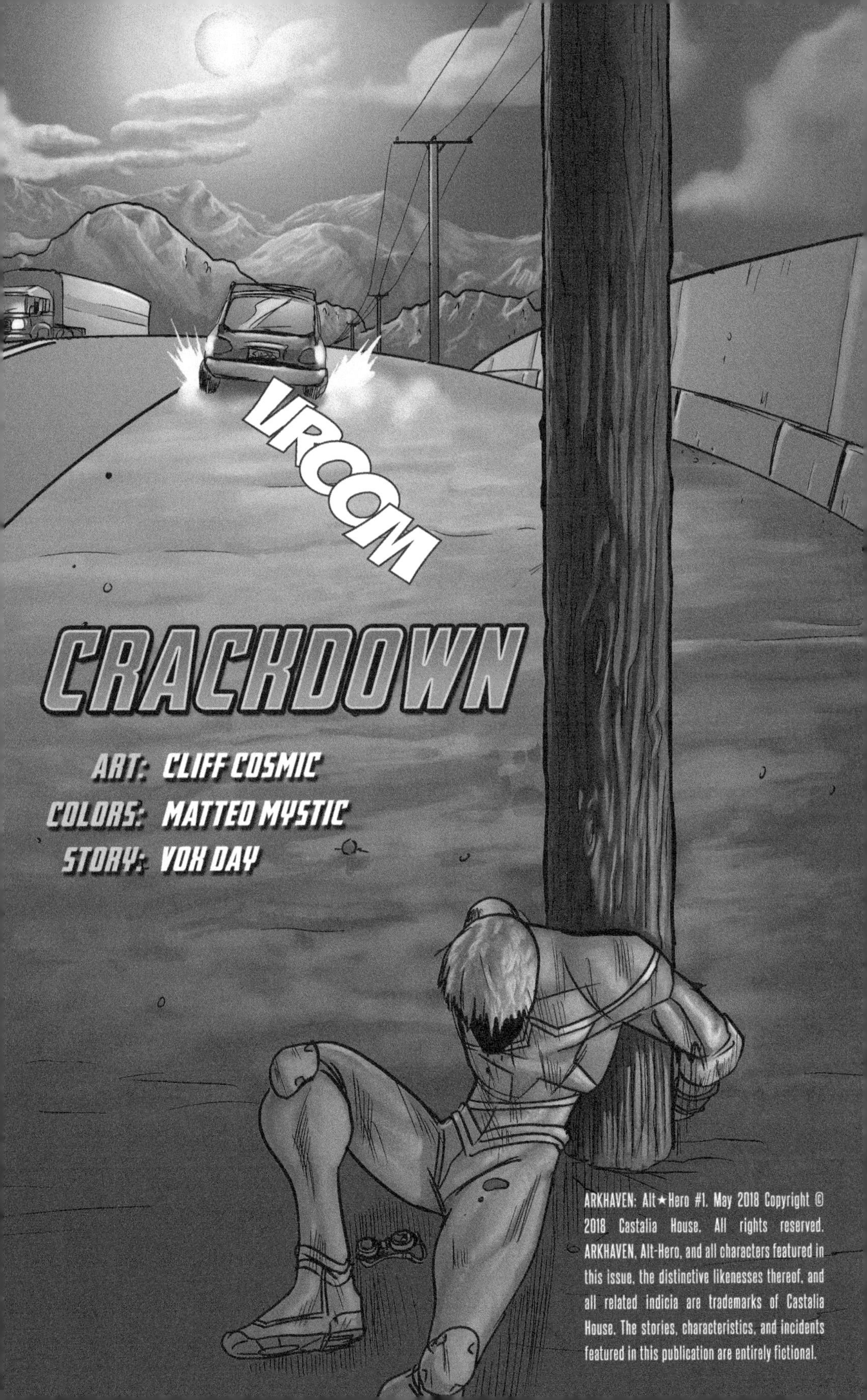
VROOM
CRACKDOWN
ART: CLIFF COSMIC
COLORS: MATTED MYSTIC
STORY: VOX DAY

CPSIA information can be obtained
at www.ICGtesting.com
Printed in the USA
LVHW06s0255040618
579467LV00008B/354/P

9 789527 303009